AF601357

First published 2017 by Dolores McGovern

ISBN: 978-1-9997922-1-3

This edition published 2017

Unsung Heroes

The Great Lady Kate

Kathleen Dempsey (née Balfe)
1893 – 1984

Affectionately known to her family and friends as Lady Kate, she has been well and truly described as a legend in her own lifetime. Through the sheer force of her will she broke down countless barriers and taboos and was a woman for all seasons. The realisation of her dream of a united Ireland may be still some time away, but I pray that God may spare us all to live to see the day.

Ray Dempsey

St Laurence's Gate

Built with the town walls in the late 13th century, this is one of the finest examples of a Barbican or Outer Defence Gate in Europe. Its title came from the Ancient Priory of St Laurence which stood outside the Gate on the site of the Cord Cemetery.

In this connection I am pleased to note that my submission which appears on Page 55 of the Boyne Valley Development Plan for the pedestrianisation of the area adjacent to the Gate to facilitate its opening to the public (utilising the proposed Palace Street / Francis Street link road, now well established as Jim Garry Way as an alternative route for traffic) has recently been approved by the local council.

UNSUNG HEROES

Second Episode

THE GREAT "LADY KATE"

by
Raymond Dempsey

Dedication

To the memory of my parents, Vincent and Kathleen Dempsey, late of Sandyford Terrace, and the Volunteer Members of the Balfe family, late of Chord Road, whose contribution to the birth of the Irish nation and their local community is remembered here with pride.

Kindred spirits they were totally committed to the greatest of all causes – Freedom. They were ordinary people who did extraordinary things and though they never wanted to be famous or listed in Who's Who, it is time these Unsung Heroes got the credit they are due.

Practical patriots in every sense of the word, I sincerely hope that the rich and varied tapestry of life, which marked their experience of one of the most turbulent periods in Irish history, is captured in this story which honours them.

The Boyne Viaduct

The Boyne Viaduct, as Kathleen would have known it in her youth, before the structural addition was made to the bridge in the early 1930s.

The Bridge was completed in 1865 at a cost of 123,000 pounds. It was for a short but glorious time after its completion, the seventh greatest bridge in the world.

The elegant Viaduct that dominates the eastern skyline and carries the main Dublin to Belfast railway line is a truly grand example of Victorian engineering at its most flamboyant.

Preface

This story of the life and times of the great Lady Kate is the latest extract from "Unsung Heroes" by the undersigned.

Based on first-hand accounts and recollections of the period by my mother Kathleen Dempsey (née Balfe) and the serving members of the Balfe family and recorded by me during their lifetimes, they also contain extracts from their diaries. All other sources are noted in the bibliography on the back page.

The "Unsung Heroes" who inspired this story are featured in some of the rather dated photographs which are from the Balfe and Dempsey family albums. The remaining photographs which feature some of the town's best known landmarks are by Des Clinton, one of Drogheda's finest exponents of the art.

These photographs, which give us a fascinating glimpse of faces and places past and present, will also be of special interest to the members of our extended families living abroad. As a visual history of their friends, the old town by the Boyne and the land of heart's desire, these intriguing images are worth more than a thousand words.

No tribute to my parents and the brave members of the Balfe family would be complete without special mention of their comrades and the other "Unsung Heroes" of the period whose courage and sense of duty in answering Ireland's call is also remembered here.

Finally, as the late Seamus Heaney has spoken of Ireland as a place where hope and history rhyme, Ray Dempsey, author and rhymer by appointment to the families concerned, once again claims poetic licence where he deems it to be appropriate in these stories.

The Balfe Sisters

Kathleen and her sisters:

Sitting from left to right

Rose, Alice (*Lil*) and Mary Anne (*Nan*)

Standing from left to right

Mary Frances and Kathleen

Introduction

Where to start in telling a story which spans a period of time in two centuries is no easy assignment, but, as always, it must be ladies first as I begin with a portrait of my mother Kathleen, affectionately known to her family and friends as Lady Kate. A founder member of Cumann na mBan, she was also Drogheda's first woman councillor. During her period of sixty years of public service, she made an outstanding contribution to the birth of the Irish nation and her local community.

Proud of her heritage and absolutely courageous in campaigning for what she believed in, her motto of "Never take no for an answer" served her well. She was a woman who always believed in speaking her mind and no one could ever accuse her of being pompous. What you saw is what you got from Lady Kate and the people loved her for it.

Like every one of us, she may have had her faults and limitations, but most of her time was spent in helping the less fortunate members of our society and, above all, she was a woman who stood by her friends.

She was born, educated, married and lived all her life in Drogheda, and yet her knowledge of human nature was universal. Despite the fact that family circumstances meant that she would never reach the second level education which she had hoped for, she exemplified the maxim that a good education at the University of life is hard to beat.

While epitaphs were not really her style I think my mother would be happy enough to be described as the Councillor who helped blaze a trail that others might follow, to make for all women a better tomorrow. This is her story.

The Balfe Brothers

Kathleen's Brothers:

Sitting from left to right

Hugh, John and Frank

Standing from left to right

Joseph and Patrick

Kathleen Dempsey (née Balfe)

A Life 1893 – 1984

Hailed by her contemporaries as one of the most inspiring and remarkable Drogheda women of the 20th century, Kathleen Balfe was born in Number 54, Chord Road, Drogheda on the 18th February 1893.

She was the seventh of ten children born to working class parents, Hugh and Rose Balfe, whose reputation as good neighbours was by that time well and truly established in the area.

While mod cons may have been noticeable by their absence, the Balfe family home was in every sense a sound and solid structure, built to stand the test of time. Unfortunately, the same standard of housing did not apply in other areas of the town and Dickensian living conditions were a daily experience for many families.

To complete the picture, Drogheda had its own workhouse (The Spike) and the Industrial school for boys which was run by the Sisters of Charity in Fair Street. Many children went to school in their bare feet and despite the affluence displayed by certain sections of the community, the 1890s were challenging times for the Balfe family and the less fortunate people of the town.

Kathleen attended the primary school run by the Presentation Nuns in Fair Street and remained in education until the age of thirteen. A highly intelligent child, one of her teachers predicted that she was a young lady destined to make a name for herself in later life.

Recalling her school days she reminded me that as a child she was very outgoing. To amuse a group of American tourists she performed an Irish dance on the viewing area at the top of St Laurence's Gate. She was rewarded for her efforts with half a crown.

The Tholsel

This fine building of local limestone, which houses a large four-faced clock, was erected in 1770 on the site of the old mediaeval, wooden Tholsel. For 130 years the present building was the centre of the Municipal Authority until the Corporation moved its offices to the Courthouse in Fair Street.

The first phase of a plan to restore the building to its former glory is now complete. As a result, the ground floor of the historic Tholsel now becomes the new home to Drogheda's Tourist Office. The success of this project speaks for itself and plans for the next phase of the development are awaited with interest.

Describing it as a day to remember, my mother said that, to the best of her knowledge and for safety reasons, no one else had ever performed an Irish dance at that high level before. It may be a first in the history of what has been recently described as the town's heritage icon, and if so, I know she would want me to claim the record on her behalf.

Unlike her sisters who worked long hours for low wages in local factories, my mother decided to opt for a trade that would stand her in good stead in later life. To this end she began an apprenticeship as a dressmaker in Davis's, a large clothing shop in West Street. Later she gained employment and completed her apprenticeship with the Martin sisters of Narrow West Street.

On Easter Monday 1916 Kathleen's father Hugh Balfe travelled to Dublin to watch a football match, oblivious to the fact that the Easter Rising was about to take place. When the rebellion began all of Dublin ground to a halt, and it took her father three days to get back home to Drogheda.

Despite the initial unpopularity of the Rising, the executions and mass deportations of those involved brought about a great wave of anti-British feeling in Ireland. Home Rule was no longer an option, and the majority of the people now wanted the creation of the independent Irish Republic that the leaders had died for.

In Drogheda on Wednesday 26th April 1916, thirteen arrests were made of suspected parties by a number of police and military under the command of D.I. Carberry. It is interesting to note that among those imprisoned for their republican sympathies on the night was Philip Monaghan, a teacher from the Chord Road, who in 1920 had the honour of being elected as the first Sinn Féin mayor of the town.

The Mayoralty House

The Mayoralty House was erected by the Corporation in 1765 to accommodate Municipal receptions and other such functions. Charles Stewart Parnell was presented with the Freedom of the Borough here in 1884 and a year later it was the venue for the foundation of the GAA in Drogheda.

Despite the name, Mayors never lived here, but great civic banquets were held quarterly at their expense. The Mayoralty house was the scene of many notable events in the history of Drogheda. In 1920 Countess Markieviez was the Guest of Honour here at a function organised by Lady Kate and the members of Cumann na mBan to mark her first official visit to the town.

In the 1900s women in Ireland, as in other countries, were demanding the right to vote and to join political parties. So the arrest of a Suffragette who was protesting at the Mansion House in Dublin did not escape the attention of the media of the day.

It was at this time that under the leadership of Maude Gonne, a British soldier's daughter, Inghinidhe na hÉireann was established. Its aims were to complete the independence of Ireland, to restore the Irish language and promote all things Irish. The majority of women who joined were young idealistic working women.

The Irish National Volunteers were founded in November 1913 in response to the Ulster Volunteer Force, which had been formed to resist the implementation of Home Rule in the North. Cumann na mBan was set up as part of the Irish Volunteer movement and joined forces with Inghinidhe na hÉireann in May 1914 to become the main women's organisation in Ireland.

Inspired by the men of 1916 and the executed leaders of the Rising, Kathleen decided to actively take part in her country's cause. In 1917, at the age of 24, she became a founder member of the Drogheda branch of Cumann na mBan.

Cumann na mBan members wore a green uniform with a slouch hat. The aims of the organisation were to advance the cause of Irish liberty and to assist in the arming and equipping of a body of Irish men for the defence of Ireland. They raised money by organising céilithe, concerts and social events for the purchase of arms and ammunition. This collection was known as the Defence of Ireland Fund.

Barlow House

One of Drogheda's most historic town houses, it was built by Ald. James Barlow in 1734. It was also the residence of Thomas Carty a former mayor of the town. It later became the R.I.C Barracks.

Refurbished to the highest possible standard in more recent years, it is now in use by the Droichead Arts Centre in conjunction with a number of other voluntary groups as a focal point for community and civic activities in the area.

Kathleen was elected the first secretary of Cumann na mBan, Drogheda branch. She was later promoted during the War of Independence to the rank of Dispatch Adjutant for the first Eastern Division, South Louth Brigade. Her sister Mary also became involved with the organisation.

In order to gain and distribute information my mother frequently visited the R.I.C Barracks at West Gate (now Barlow House) disguised as the mother of Republican prisoners. But in due course her luck ran out when, much to the amusement of the R.I.C. members present, the constable for the area identified her as young Kathleen Balfe from the Chord Road coming to visit her 71 year old son.

With her options now limited and realising that on this occasion discretion was the better part of valour, Kathleen decided that this was one time when flattery would get her everywhere.

So to prove she could cod them and save herself harm,
She praised their appearance and turned on her charm,
Till a certain old Sergeant whose first name was Ken,
Said "Go down to the cells, girl, and talk to your men!"

Guns and Roses

Another of Lady Kate's exploits is the occasion when she carried a machine gun, concealed under her great coat, as she walked and cycled from Drogheda to Ballapousta. It was a dangerous journey and she was forced to hide in ditches along the route to avoid being detected by the authorities who were patrolling the roads.

Looking back on it she said that she would do it all again if she had to. The fact that the gun was later used for a very successful raid on Ardee Barracks by Republicans made her twenty-six mile round trip well worth while. Defying the forces of the Crown was the name of the game, and a bouquet of red roses from her beloved Vincent on her return made her day complete.

Pictured here is Lady Kate's handsome brother, Captain Frank Balfe, 1895 – 1965

Following a distinguished career as a member of the Flying Squad during the War of Independence, Frank joined the Free State Army on the foundation of the State. A man of many talents, his early promotion to the rank of Captain came as no surprise to those who knew him. For a pen picture of Captain Frank Balfe see page 23 of the Journal of the Old Drogheda Society 2009.

Encouraged by Kathleen's audacious example, three of her brothers Hugh, Frank and Joseph joined the Volunteers and in due course became members of a crack IRA Flying Column. Towards the end of 1920, the IRA formed these streamlined units of heavily armed men, who moved through the countryside making sudden attacks on isolated R.I.C. Barracks.

These guerrilla attacks by the IRA on British forces throughout Ireland forced the British Government to respond. They did so by bringing the Black and Tans into Ireland. So called because of the mixture of Police and Army uniforms which they wore, they were a notoriously indisciplined force and hunting down the IRA was their order of the day.

In order to carry out their ruthless campaign of counter terrorism against Irish Revolutionaries they would stop at nothing. Indiscriminate destruction, thieving and looting were par for the course as they went in search of evidence that would connect the members of the household to the IRA.

By now the activities of Kathleen and her brothers had aroused the suspicion of the local force, and as a result their home at number 54 Chord Road was a house constantly raided, ransacked and fired on by the notorious Black and Tans.

On one occasion my mother recalled the Tans, acting on information, raided the Balfe family home in the early hours of the morning. She had several dispatches of importance on the premises at the time. She could not let them fall into their hands under any circumstances. So when they were ransacking the front of the house, she sneaked out in the darkness and hid them under a large stone in the garden.

Pictured here is Kathleen Balfe standing at the old footbridge at Laytown in the 1920s. It is interesting to note that a scene from the film Michael Collins, who was her hero, was shot at this location many years later.

Among the important news reports found among her papers after her death was the following extract from the report of the death of Michael Collins, in the Irish Independent dated Wednesday August 23rd 1922:

The following official bulletin was issued from Army Headquarters last night – General Michael Collins, Commander in Chief of the Army, was killed in an ambush by irregulars in Béal na mBláth between Macroom and Bandon last night (Tuesday).

Irish people all over the world were stunned by the news. Bowed down by horror and dismay, they lamented the grievous loss of General Michael Collins, the bravest of the brave. On another occasion Kathleen narrowly escaped death when the Tans, having failed to find the dispatches they were looking for, opened fire through the kitchen window. By the grace of God she had just left the room to answer a knock on the front door by a member of the Auxiliary Division with whom the Tans worked. Otherwise, she said, she might not be around to tell the story.

In the eighteen months that followed there was hardly a week when the Balfe household was not the subject of nocturnal raids by the Black and Tans. On one occasion, drunk and out of control members of a raiding party threatened to burn down the house, if the information they were seeking was not made available to them. Thanks to the intervention of a local R.I.C. man who knew the family, they were persuaded to move on. In July 1921 came the great news that a truce has been arranged between the crown forces and the Volunteers to enable negotiations to take place between the British Government and representatives of the Irish Government established by the Dáil. Instructions were then issued from the headquarters of the Irish Volunteers ordering the suspension of hostilities.

The treaty was passed in the Dáil on 7th January 1922. Kathleen as a Collins supporter felt that Ireland had witnessed enough bloodshed and that the treaty was a stepping stone to freedom. In 1922 the evacuation of the British Troops from the 26 counties began, while the Black and Tans and the R.I.C. were disbanded.

Long before the last of the British forces had left, however, the strain between the Free State authorities and the opponents of the Treaty had reached breaking point. As a result the anti-treaty side continued to fight. This in turn triggered off what was later described as one of the most tragic episodes in Ireland's history.

Millmount

This splendid rainbow crowned view of the refurbished Martello Tower, that replaced the old fortification which had been considerably damaged by shelling during the 1922 Civil War, was taken by local photographer Des Clinton.

Spectacular views of the town and surrounding countryside may be obtained from the tower which is now considered to be the crowning glory of the Millmount Complex. Thanks to the enterprising committee of the Old Drogheda Society who manage it, the houses, the excellent museum and Millmount tower itself are now a restoration and preservation project of which the Municipal Authority can feel justifiably proud.

The Civil War which commenced on the 28th June, 1922 devastated some parts of the country and claimed the lives of many brave men and women. Drogheda by comparison escaped lightly. While there were some minor skirmishes in the town during that period, including the bombardment of Millmount, no serious casualties were reported up to the time of the cease fire in April 1923.

Civil War has been described as one of the worst kind of wars that can befall any country. This was certainly true in the case of Drogheda and like many other Irish towns suffered badly because of its after effects. Indeed the bitterness and hatred engendered among many families and friends on both sides during that period of Irish history took many generations to fade from the scene.

There were, of course, exceptions to the rule and Lady Kate was one of them. Despite the political bitterness of the Civil War divisions she refused to listen to personal criticism of the local Republican leadership. Explaining her position she said that she could not find it in her heart to do so, as not so long before they had fought together in a common cause for a freedom that was dearly won.

Fate had decreed that some of her best friends were on the other side. Quoting the old adage "that it is human to err and divine to forgive", she said that it was better to learn to live with our differences than to die for them. It was typical of her that she won the respect and affection of men from both sides of the civil war divide. Although she may not have realised it at the time, her efforts under the heading of peace and reconciliation would not be forgotten by men and women of good will on the other side when it mattered most.

St Peter's Church, Drogheda (St Oliver Plunkett Memorial Church)

The steady stream of visitors who come here to pray at the Shrine of St Oliver Plunkett make it one of the most frequently visited churches in the Diocese of Armagh.

Widely regarded as one of the finest churches of its type in Ireland, its 221 foot spire makes it one of Drogheda's most prominent landmarks.

It was in this magnificent church that Kathleen married Vincent Dempsey on the 28th November 1923, a date she always described as the happiest day of her life.

Parents who always treasured the old certainties of the religion in which they had been brought up, they will always be remembered with great love and affection by their family and friends.

As the new State became firmly established something approaching normal life resumed. Civic guards (who would be later named as An Garda Siochána) took over Dublin Castle from the departing British Army unit. My father Vincent Dempsey who had been a judge in the old Sinn Féin courts was appointed as the first Court Registrar for the area and the best was yet to come.

In due course he married the love of his life Kathleen Balfe, who had held a senior position in Cumann na mBan and with whom he had become romantically involved during his period of service as the Director of Intelligence for the First Eastern Division, South Louth Brigade. They were among the first of the young couples to move into the new houses in Sandyford Terrace. In the happy years that followed they were blessed with five children - three boys Vincent, Raymond and Aidan, and two girls Gertie and Deirdre.

As the story so far will confirm, things had not always been easy for Kathleen Balfe. But in the years that followed, the Dempsey family, now in residence in what later became known as "*the house on the hill*", had enjoyed more than its fair share of happiness, for which Kathleen thanked the Lord.

Dark shadows fall in the lives of us all and with the passing of time the wisdom of my mother's words in the aftermath of the Civil War in Drogheda was clearly demonstrated, when my father died just a few weeks short of his 40th birthday. It was a devastating blow for the family. But thanks to my mother's unselfish commitment and unconditional love and support for her family *(which included nursing me at home when I contracted polio)* we survived.

The Dempsey family, Sandyford Terrace, including Vincent senior and junior, Kathleen, Deirdre and Gertie, with Raymond sitting on his father's knee, on the occasion of Aidan's christening celebrations.

Kathleen and Vincent on a well-deserved holiday break in Connemara

And in our time of mourning for the Dad we loved so much,
came the unexpected kindness that would prove a healing touch,
when some men they called irregulars in that best forgotten rift,
showed why true and trusted friendship is still such a precious gift.

Thanks to their efforts ownership of the family home in Sandyford Terrace was secured and other outstanding items were dealt with. An offer from friends of my father to fund our further education if and when we wished to avail of it followed. The kindness of all concerned was something for which my mother was eternally grateful.

But the day-to-day business of a young widow trying to manage with five young children, on an income which was fifteen times less than what she had been used to, still had to be faced up to. Kathleen enlisted the help of her sister Mary to look after us, falling back on her skills as a dressmaker to supplement her income and manage she did.

Looking back on it, my mother was the rock who was always there for us in good times and bad. A mixture of discipline and tender loving care, she maintained, was the secret of her success and with a little help from the Christian Brothers and the Presentation Nuns *(with whom she would agree to disagree from time to time)* she reared a family of whom she could feel justly proud.

Her achievements were remembered in 1941 when she became Drogheda's first woman to receive a Military Service medal and a pension of 12s6p (62 ½ c) per week for the role she played in the fight for Irish independence. Her brothers and her sister Mary also received military service medals around the same time.

Gertie spent her life fighting for Justice

Pictured here on the viewing area of Millmount Martello Tower is the late Councillor Gertie Shields (née Dempsey) making her first official visit to her native town, following her election as Cathaoirleach of Balbriggan Town Council in July 2001

A founder member of Mothers Against Drunk Drivers, it is no exaggeration to say that Gertie almost singlehandedly changed the public's attitude to drink driving, especially amongst the young.

A Road Safety Ambassador for the Road Safety Authority, Gertie's lasting legacy is saving countless lives and making Ireland a safer place for all.

During the 1950s Kathleen, who was a founder member and first lady member of Cumann na nGaedheal (later Fine Gael) at local level, played an important part in re-organising the party in Drogheda. Her diary also confirms that the branch meetings of the party were held in her home until suitable premises could be located.

Despite the fact that she was a senior member of the party from its inception, Kathleen could never be considered a hardliner. Indeed supporters of other political parties would be first to acknowledge her outstanding qualities of integrity, friendliness and impartiality, characteristics which were not affected by political difference or affiliation.

In 1961 she made her first bid to end the male domination on Drogheda Corporation, but failed by a margin of only six votes to do so. For Kathleen seeing her chances of a seat on the council fail by a mere handful of votes was just a temporary setback. By any yardstick it was a remarkable achievement, and with the help of God, she would live to fight another day.

The Second Ban

In 1966 Kathleen who was then President of the Local Housewives' Association was invited to become a member of the Drogheda Commemoration Committee to help plan the town's jubilee celebrations of the 1916 Rising. At the meeting she proposed a motion to include soccer and rugby representation in the celebrations.

On Parade

Members of Drogheda Cumann na mBan including the late Kathleen Dempsey,*(front of photo nearest the camera)*

With members of Cumann na mBan on the occasion of Lady Kate's 75th birthday celebrations.

Because of the ban on foreign games that still applied at the time, support for the motion from many of the GAA representatives present was not forthcoming. The only GAA man to support the motion was the late Ald. James Whelan who at the time was Chairman of the O'Raghallaigh's Gaelic Football Club. He said he was taking the same stand as Mrs Dempsey, as he believed that having made a call for unity all views should be represented on the committee. Ald. Whelan also had a military service medal at the time.

The defeat of the motion on a show of hands received widespread coverage in the local and national newspapers. In the interviews that followed, Kathleen declared that she was standing by what she said at the meeting. because she felt that those who played soccer and rugby were no less Irish than those who didn't, and should not be barred from the celebrations.

Cumann na mBan fought for freedom for everybody, not just for a section of the people. So indeed did Pearse and Connolly and all that gallant band. They fought even for those Dubliners who mocked and jeered them when, in defeat, they were led as prisoners through the streets of our capital city.

The proclamation of 1916, she declared, demanded that all the children of the nation be cherished equally. That means equally and all the children - even the supposedly bold ones. " It is a curious thing," she said, " that fifty years ago I was fighting for freedom to play any games or join any organisation, and today I have to do the same thing."

Another first for Lady Kate

This picture shows the former town clerk Brendan Hoey presenting the Lady Mayoress Chain to Olive Dempsey at a reception to mark the occasion in the Star and Crescent Centre, Drogheda

It was Lady Kate's idea that a special chain should be presented to the spouse of the town's first citizen, a spouse who gave service above and beyond the call of duty during the mayor's term of office. The fact that Raymond's wife Olive was the first Lady Mayoress to wear the chain, sponsored by the Drogheda Traders Association, was a source of great joy for Kathleen.

A Happy Medium

A woman of great foresight Kathleen made many predictions that were to become reality in later years. In 1967, when a woman councillor was virtually unheard of in a male dominated council, she predicted her own election as the first lady member of what was then referred to as Drogheda Corporation, since it was established by Royal Charter in 1194.

She also predicted that Drogheda would have its first woman mayor before the end of the century. This duly came to pass with the election of Councillor Maria O'Brien - Campbell as the first woman Mayor of Drogheda in 1998. A second term of office followed in 2004 and on both occasions I think it is only fair to say that Mayor Maria did us proud.

My mother's diary also confirmed that she was in no doubt that a suitably qualified member of Mná na hÉireann would be elected President and occupy Áras an Uachtaráin before the end of the 20th Century. Here again she got it right with the election of Mary Robinson in 1990, followed by Mary McAleese in 1997.

She is also on record as the first woman member of Drogheda Corporation to call for and predict the abolition of the GAA ban on foreign games.

Last but by no means least, she also predicted that two of her family members would follow her into politics. This came to pass. The rare combination of a brother and sister in politics was achieved - with my election as a member of the Municipal Council from 1974 to 1999, followed by the election of my sister Gertie as a member (and later Cathaoirleach) of Balbriggan Town Commissioners (now officially referred to as Balbriggan Town Council) in 1994.

Kathleen (third from left, front row) with members and associate members of Cumann na mBan at their annual soirée in the Central Hotel, Peter Street, Drogheda.

Raymond with the Mayor of the day Ald. T. Murphy at the unveiling of the plaque in the Council Chamber, erected by the Corporation of Drogheda, to commemorate the election on the 28th day of June 1967 of Cllr. Kathleen Dempsey, as the first woman member of the Municipal Council since it was established by Royal Charter in 1194.

Historical Breakthrough

In the 1967 local elections as a Fine Gael candidate, the seventy-four year old Kathleen marked up a historical milestone with her election as Drogheda Corporation's first woman councillor.

Her historic victory in becoming the first woman member of the local authority received great coverage in the local and national press. In an Irish Independent interview dated Thursday 6th July 1967, Kathleen said:

"The housewives came out and voted for me and, now that the barrier of women on the council has been overcome, I hope to see more of them contesting the election next time around."

In another statement to the Housewives' Association thanking them for their support, she said that while her election was a step in the right direction, much more remained to be done before her vision of more women in politics would be realised. The present system, she said, worked against women, and political parties must now accept that women are electable and act accordingly.

It was another first for Lady Kate. However, it was twenty-one years later before the plaque in the Council Chamber, which honours her memory and records for posterity her outstanding achievement, was unveiled by the mayor of the day, Ald. Tommy Murphy, on the 28th June 1988.

Her first Corporation meeting passed off without incident and on the Town Clerk's advice Kathleen decided to listen and learn for a while. It was a learning curve that would stand her in good stead, and soon she would be making her presence felt as a fully fledged member of the Council.

Pictured above are the Cumann na mBan Military Service and 1916 commemoration medals of Kathleen Dempsey (née Balfe) and of Mary Balfe, who was also a prominent member of Cumann na mBan during the War of Independence.

They form part of the Dempsey / Balfe Collection of Military Service Medals and Memorabilia of the period. This includes the original order under the restoration of Order in Ireland regulations confirming that Hugh Balfe of 54 Chord Road, Drogheda be interned in Ballykinler Camp, and remain there until further notice, signed by the appropriate Officer of the Black Watch dated 9th February 1921.

Hugh who was interned in five different detention camps during this period kept a diary. This diary includes unpublished verses composed by fellow prisoners including future National Leaders, such as the former President Seán T. Ó Ceallaigh, the former Minister for Defence General Richard Mulcahy, Tadhg Barry and others.

Drogheda's first woman Councillor was guest of honour at a victory celebration following the first official meeting of the new Corporation. It was a night to remember and a delighted Lady Kate listened as tributes were paid to her in poetry and song.

Many of the town's top artists put on a show for her and the following is an extract from a rhyme which I wrote and dedicated to the new councillor to mark the occasion:

So on this special date as we honour Lady Kate,
And engrave her name on civic history's page,
The trail that she has blazed can never be erased,
As equal rights for lady members come of age.

In due course Kathleen received notice of her first public engagement. With it came the problem of how to cope with a ceremonial robe of office which had been made with men in mind. Breaking into a preserve that was strictly male up to then was a challenge, but not an insurmountable one for the steely Lady Kate.

So with a procession and her first public appearance walking in state looming large, she decided to take appropriate action. Wondering what condition the robes might be in she headed straight for headquarters in Fair Street to find out for herself. In due course she was pointed in the right direction and told to ask for Mike who would sort the problem out for her there and then.

On entering the council chamber (where robes were kept at the time) Kathleen saw Mike who appeared to be making entries in a diary. A straight talking member of the staff he pulled no punches in answering her questions and adding a bit of additional information for good measure.

A Night to Remember

Some members of the Dempsey family and friends who attended the Meeting on the 28th June 1988, when the Plaque which honours Lady Kate, and records for posterity her outstanding achievement, was unveiled in the Council Chamber by the Mayor of the day Alderman Tommy Murphy

And when enquiring from Mike what the robes might be like,
He said Ma'm, looking up from his notes,
They're like what Sarsfield wore in the dear days of yore,
or that famous ad for Quaker Oats!

Then without further ado he handed her a damp and decrepit green robe and accessories that smelt of smoke and stale beer. It had been worn by a tall and overweight former member of the Council. With the best will in the world it looked like a sixties edition of rent a tent. However Mike assured her that reports that certain members had slept in them when under the influence and used them as blankets on their beds in the winter were all true.

Heading for home, Kathleen decided that all things considered a sprinkling of D.D.T. for the outfit would be top of her list of priorities. This would be followed by a visit to IMCO (famous for their cleaning and dying at the time). Clearly it was a case of fumigation or consternation as far as she was concerned.

Cleaning up the outfit and reducing the outsized robe to fit her in less than a week would be no easy assignment. But necessity is the mother of invention and in order to make sure that she did not miss out on the big occasion this was the challenge that faced her:

An old dribbler and hat, three cornered at that,
With gold braid that was all hanging loose,
And a pot bellied robe she would just have to probe,
Then try to convert to her use.

But this was one time just to finish my rhyme,
When her trade did become a godsend,
And when walking in state, green became Lady Kate,
For she did get it right in the end.

This photo was taken during a visit to the Marian Shrine in Lourdes with members of the Cystic Fibrosis Association of Ireland during Raymond's term of office as Mayor.

It was an experience of a lifetime and the unselfish commitment, unconditional love and support of the parents for the children affected by this disease is something that will be engraved in our hearts as long as we live.

Following her election Kathleen concentrated on less military roles. As President and one of the founder members of the local Housewives' Association, she was more aware of the feelings of local women than most, and she put her knowledge to good use in the Corporation chamber.

One of the town's most popular politicians of the period, she was also described as the can-do member of the Corporation during her term of office. Totally committed to every project which she undertook, her ability to connect with people of all walks of life with ease set her apart from many other politicians and was the secret of her success.

Housing and the problems faced by old age pensioners were high on her list of priorities. As the champion of the under-privileged she also pressed for better playing facilities for young people, and better housing for those on the waiting list. She was also a prime mover in one of the first schemes for free fuel for pensioners in the area.

Never afraid to take on male opponents in or out of the council chamber, she was held in high esteem by both sides of the political divide. She was an original mould breaker and a true community activist. Her personal commitment to the welfare of her constituents and to her many other worthy causes never wavered.

Despite some wounding by the slings and arrows of outrageous fortune in her lifetime, less ordinary Lady Kate was a born optimist and a fair minded woman. While holding firm convictions on religion, politics and many other things, she allowed the same rights of opinion to others and bore malice to none.

Names Carved with pride on Memorial Plaque

Close-up shot of the wording on the commemorative plaque erected by Raymond at 54 Chord Road, Drogheda, the former home of the Balfe Family. It was unveiled by Hubert Murphy, Editor, Drogheda Independent on the 21st April 2016 to mark the Centenary Celebrations of the 1916 Rising.

In her late seventies Kathleen had the opportunity to contest the mayoral election, but with the wisdom of her years she decided to decline the offer. Being mayor, she said, was a job for a younger person and it was her hope that a member of her family would in due course achieve that distinction.

Kathleen retired from public life in 1974 aged 81. In her remarkable lifetime she assisted in Ireland's fight for freedom, was a champion of the under privileged, and became one of the few voices for women in local and national politics.

Lady Kate's famous green robe which she altered herself was later presented to the late Moira Corcoran, a founder member of the Old Drogheda Society. At the family's request it was agreed that it would be included in the collection of memorabilia of the town's civic history which is on display in Millmount museum.

In 1974, Raymond succeeded his mother as the member for the Laurence Gate Ward. It was a step in the right direction, but Lady Kate always believed that the same God who helped her before was ready and willing to help her once more. Her prayers were answered with Raymond's election as Mayor in 1980 / 1981, something which she described as a dream come true and one of those very special moments in time.

It is a perfect example of what can be achieved against all the odds when the will to succeed is really there, and a reminder that the nature of our attitude towards circumstantial things determines our acceptance of the problems that life brings.

Ó Ghlúin go Glúin
From one generation to the next

Little Ella Dempsey Moore pictured at the unveiling of the Memorial Plaque at 54 Chord Road, in honour of her Great Grandmother Kathleen Dempsey and the other unsung heroes who served with distinction during the War of Independence.

Even at the age of 90 Lady Kate still maintained a very keen interest in the affairs of the town. As always her support for the women's rights movement and the young people of Drogheda was as solid as ever. She had a setback in the early months of the following year which left her housebound for the first time in her life. It was a real shock to her system and though the visits she planned were not to be, she accepted God's will with serenity.

It takes the bitter and sweet to make our lives complete and my mother died peacefully in what was then the family home in Sandyford Terrace on the 14th September 1984 aged 91 years. In his homily the late Bishop James Lennon said that while we were united in grief at her passing, her funeral mass was also a celebration of her long life as a great Drogheda woman of her time and one of the "Unsung Heroes" of her native town.

Life goes on, however, and in the time that has passed since her death the contrast between the Ireland of her lifetime and the country now set to make the boom and bust years of the first decade of the 21st century such a challenging time for all of us is almost beyond our comprehension.

We may live in a world where the only constant in the relentless march of time is change. But thanks be to God the indomitable spirit of Lady Kate and the brave members of the Balfe and Dempsey clans lives on in the hearts and minds of their families. We are inheritors of a tradition of which we can all feel justifiably proud

'The Legacy of Lady Kate - 50 years on'

I HOPE next year will see a special event, maybe a seminar or broad discussion, on women in politics and how a Drogheda lady changed the face of local politics all of 50 years ago.

In 1967, Kathleen Dempsey (Balfe) created history by becoming the first woman to be elected onto the then Drogheda Corporation.

But I wonder has Kathleen's legacy been a success. Have women become empowered to join the political game. Only this year Imelda Munster enjoyed her own moment when she was elected a TD - the first female for Sinn Fein in the constituency.

But I doubt if anyone could match a trailblazer like Kathleen Dempsey. An Irish nationalist, she was a founder member of Cumann na mBan in Drogheda

Born Kathleen Balfe in Drogheda to Hugh and Rose Balfe in 1893, she had nine siblings many of whom were also involved in the Irish nationalist movement. Her sister Mary was the youngest daughter and also a member of Cumann na mBan. Her brothers Hugh, Frank and Joseph joined the Irish Republican Army and were members of a Flying Column during the War of Independence.

She married Vincent Dempsey who died in 1937 leaving her to raise their family with her sister's help. The Dempseys had five children, including daughters Gertie Shields, who established the campaigning group Mothers Against Drunk Driving in Ireland, and Deirdre, and sons Vincent, Aidan, and Raymond, who has been mayor of Drogheda.

She joined the Cumann na mBan in 1917. From 1919-1921 she was involved in the War of Independence. Her role involved visiting prisoners in the local Royal Irish Constabulary barracks and at least once carrying a machine gun to be used for an attack on the Ardee barracks. A Fine Gael supporter, Balfe ran for and was elected to the Drogheda Corporation in 1967. She retired at the age of 81 and died in 1984.

So, the 'Legacy of Lady Kate' - 50 years on' - sounds as good a title as any.

Of few women could it be said more truly we shall never see her like again, ní bheidh a leithéid ann arís. It is for that reason I sincerely hope that "Unsung Heroes" and this story, which provides a new insight into the life of a woman who made an outstanding contribution to the birth of the Irish nation and her local community, will not be forgotten when the definitive history of that period in Drogheda is recorded for posterity.

Whether or not my wish will be granted only time can tell. Bearing in mind that on an island where begrudgery has been elevated to an art form by some people, the fact that in death Kathleen Dempsey had even more admirers than when she was elected as Drogheda Corporation's first woman member speaks for itself.

Her funeral with full military honours attracted a large attendance including the representatives of Church and State led by the Mayor and members of Drogheda Corporation. It was the end of an era and the grief of the family as the last post was sounded was shared by her many friends.

Lady Kate is buried with her beloved husband Vincent and son Aidan in the family plot in St Peter's Cemetery, near members of the Balfe clan, where they rest in peace in the sure and certain hope of the resurrection.

And so with justice now done these heroes unsung,
Have well earned their eternal reward,
May they all rest in peace where joys never cease
Ever safe in house of the Lord.

Ray Dempsey

The Commemorative Scroll which Raymond was proud to unveil on the Dempsey plot in St Peter's Cemetery to mark the Centenary Celebrations of the 1916 Rising.

REMEMBRANCE

This memorial is to record for posterity the service rendered to the State by Vincent & Kathleen Dempsey, Sandyford Terrace, by the Irish Volunteer Members of the Balfe Family, Chord Road, and the other unsung heroes who served with distinction during the War of Independence.

It also commemorates the outstanding achievement of the above named Kathleen Dempsey who, on the 28th day of June, 1967, marked up a historical milestone with her election as the first woman member of the Municipal Council, since it was established by Royal Charter in 1194.

Kindred spirits who were totally committed to the greatest of all causes 'Freedom', may they rest in peace in the sure and certain hope of the resurrection.

Their courage and vision shed
a light bright and reassuring.

Ray Dempsey

About the Author

Ray Dempsey

A man of many talents, Ray will be best remembered as the former Mayor who was responsible for first proposing the idea for the restoration of the Millmount Complex, a project of which the Municipal Council can feel justly proud. The Make Drogheda Beautiful Campaign, one of the most successful community projects in living memory, was also his brain child. A son of the late Vincent and Kathleen Dempsey whose contribution to the birth of the Irish nation and their local community is now well documented, Ray's pedigree, in the words of the late Peter Casey, is very good on each side both in national and local affairs.

Acknowledgements – Sources

To Olive – my good wife and the love of my life, to whom I dedicate these stories. To my ever helpful niece, Valerie Dempsey for her computer skills. To my cousin Margaret McKeown for her help in researching the life and times of Captain Frank Balfe 1895 – 1965 which appeared in the first episode of "Unsung Heroes". Spare a thought here for my very talented cousin Dolores McGovern whose art work on the Plaque and Scroll has been the subject of much favourable comment. Last but by no means least a special word of thanks is due to my nephew Seán Ó Briain who helped with the editing of the complete work.

Photographs

The outstanding photographs of some of the town's historical landmarks are a perfect example of the work of master photographer, Des Clinton and speak for themselves. The rather dated photographs are from the Dempsey / Balfe Family Albums. In this connection a special word of thanks is due to Paul Connor, Drogheda Independent, Jimmy Weldon whose ability to capture the life and soul of his subject in any shot is once again demonstrated in his latest edition of Jimmy's People. To the staff of the Print Enlargement Services of Maher's Pharmacy, West Street and CTI Business Solutions, North Quay for their work in upgrading, reproducing and enlarging these photographs.

The sources used include extracts from interviews which I conducted with the serving members of the Balfe and Dempsey families during their lifetime. This story also contains extracts from interviews which I conducted with Paul Murphy, dated 10th August 1999, 16th February 2000 and 23rd March 2000.

The following newspapers and guides were used for dates and verification of facts:

Drogheda Independent	April 1916 / September 1984 June 1999 / December 2001
Evening Herald	10th February 1966
Irish Independent	23rd August 1922 / 6th July 1967
Evening Press	28th December 1968
The Local News	September 1984
Drogheda Leader	6th October 2010
Discover Drogheda M.E.T.	
St Peter's Church Drogheda – A Short Guide	

Epilogue

The moral of Kate's story is plain - failure means you can try again,
For despair, my friends, is just the devil's bait,
So when it seems you just can't win, and you're tempted to give in,
Put your trust in God and think of Lady Kate.

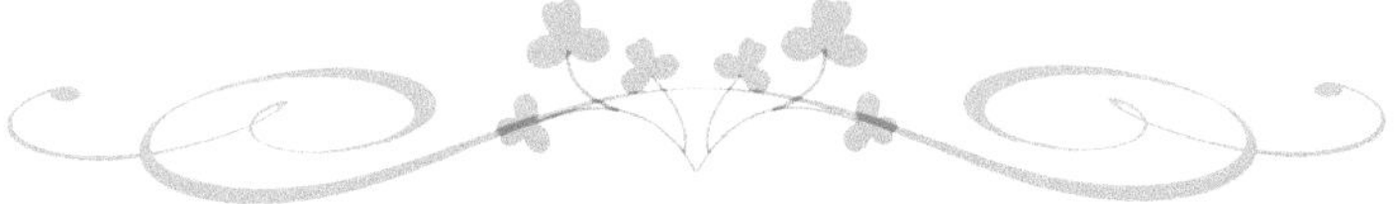

Ray Dempsey
11th August 2017

www.ingramcontent.com/pod-product-compliance
Ingram Content Group UK Ltd.
Pitfield, Milton Keynes, MK11 3LW, UK
UKHW060121300726
14090UKWH00002B/297